THE BROCKHAM… RY

gu…
La…guage
of Dreams

BROCKHAMPTON PRESS
LONDON

This edition published 1996 by Brockhampton Press,
a member of Hodder Headline PLC Group

ISBN 1 86019 273 4

Printed and bound in the UK

Why Do We Dream?

Consciousness and unconsciousness

Although it is not known exactly why we dream, psychoanalysis has recognized that the unconscious has an important role to play. However, this in itself is not terribly helpful as scientists have never been entirely certain as to where consciousness ends and unconsciousness begins. Indeed, the two frequently overlap and there can really be no clear distinction between them.

We may, perhaps, accept that to be conscious means to be awake, aware of our surroundings and in control of our actions. But this does not take into account the fact that much goes on around us in our waking state of which we are generally not aware, or only aware of on a 'less conscious' level. For instance, we may be walking along a busy street, deep in thought, and be completely unaware of the noise of the traffic all around us, until something like a car horn blast, or the sound of a collision, alerts us to it.

Furthermore, we do not need to concentrate all the time on moving our legs in order that we might keep on walking, nor do we generally need to concentrate hard on walking in a straight line in order that we might not veer off the course into the road.

Similarly, while we are asleep and are ostensibly 'unconscious', our brains are obviously extremely active. Although we are usually unaware of much of this activity (such as the continuing control over the function of our major organs), dreams are a manifestation of this activity and are indeed often extremely vivid. Therefore it would seem that the brain is capable of organizing our consciousness into several levels at all times.

The physiological manifestation of the unconscious is also a grey area. However, it is known that a structure situated in the brain stem, known as the reticular formation acts as an activator for other parts of the brain and may play a part in defining the unconscious. All sensory pathways are linked to the reticular activating system (RAS), so that when a sense receptor is stimulated this also triggers the reticular system, 'awakening' the brain so that it is fully able to respond to the messages from the senses.

Sleep

Sleep is essential for the repair of the body and for cell regeneration. People deprived of sleep for lengthy periods generally become quite unwell. However, it is a complicated process, which has been the subject of much research. Broadly speaking, the average night's sleep consists of four or five distinct stages.

1 During stage one, the sleeper begins to relax and will drift in and out of a dozing sleep from which he or she is easily awakened.
2 In stage two, the individual is asleep but can still be easily roused by minor disturbances.
3 By stage three, a state of deep relaxation is reached, and it becomes very difficult to wake the sleeper. During this stage, the eyes often move from side to side.
4 In stage four, 80 per cent of the daily output of growth

hormone is released, which helps in the process of repairing body tissues.

The sleeper then proceeds in reverse through the stages, but instead of waking completely after returning to stage 1, he or she will enter a different stage (stage 5), known as REM (rapid eye movement) sleep. It is during this phase that most dreaming occurs. The whole cycle from stages 1–4 and back again takes about 90–100 minutes. During the average night's sleep the cycle will repeat itself four or five times.

REM Sleep

REM sleep takes it's name from the characteristic eye movements that take place during this stage. Sleepers who are wakened during this phase will report that they have been dreaming. Research has shown that during REM sleep, the body's major muscle groups seem to be paralysed. This is thought to occur in order to prevent injury or uncontrolled movement during sleep.

The length of REM sleep increases with each cycle. Therefore, the longest period of REM sleep and dreaming occurs in the last third of the night. A sleeper whose REM is disrupted will automatically try to increase the time spent in REM sleep the next night to compensate. This may indicate that REM sleep, and therefore dreaming is essential for wellbeing. Some dreaming does take place outwith REM sleep, but it tends to be much less vivid and somewhat mundane. A sleeper who is wakened during one of these dreams may report that he or she has been 'thinking' rather than dreaming.

Getting the Most from Sleep

In order to dream well, it is advisable to follow a few simple rules:

1 Decide your optimum amount of sleep and stick to it as much as possible. Most adults require six and a half to eight and a half hours of sleep nightly, but some can get by on as little as five hours. A few will need ten hours.

Experiment with varying lengths of sleep. When you have decided how much you need (based on assessment of work performance, levels of irritability and plain tiredness through the day), you should aim to be in bed approximately half an hour before the period of sleep commences.

2 What you have consumed in the hours preceding sleep will directly affect the nature and quality of your dreams. If your digestion is working overtime while you sleep, your dreams may be affected. It is wise therefore to avoid eating wind-producing foods such as raw vegetables, or foods that are high in fat content immediately before you go to bed.

Some drugs, such as caffeine and alcohol, affect the time it takes to fall asleep and the quality of sleep thereafter. Similarly, sleeping tablets seem to suppress REM sleep, which is so vital to our wellbeing.

3 Do as much as possible to eliminate noise and discomfort in the immediate sleeping environment. The immediate environment can affect your dreams; many people will have experienced dreaming that the telephone is ringing, or a fire alarm is sounding, only

to find later that they have slept through the noise of the alarm; or they may have dreamt of being tied down only to wake up and find that their bedclothes have become so entangled that they can hardly move.

Try to adopt a relaxed routine in the hour before bedtime. If the brain is over-active as the head hits the pillow, it will take some time to drift off into a deep, untroubled sleep.

Record Your Dreams

It is always a good idea to keep a notebook right beside the bed if you want to record your dreams. In this way, you can make a note of your impressions the moment you wake up, before the intrusions of the day cloud or distort your memory.

When people report that they have not dreamt, it is not necessarily the case; it may be that events immediately upon waking (perhaps the alarm clock, the children careering all around, the realization that they might be late for work, etc) were so intrusive that memories of dreams were pushed out of their minds. For this reason, try, if at all possible, to train yourself to wake early, before alarm clocks sound and before household noises disturb you. You will be more likely to be able to recall your dreams in a peaceful environment.

Interpreting Dreams

Our dreams can often be fantastic, terrifying and hard to comprehend because they do not seem to be contained by the rules of our everyday lives. Some of the most bizarre and disturbing distortions of reality are commonly experienced by dreamers, and the interpretation of these distortions has been given much attention by some eminent psychologists and researchers. Sigmund Freud (1856-1939), the father of psychoanalysis, believed that the unconscious uses symbols in dreams that represent real emotions and feelings. Alfred Adler (1870-1937), originally a follower of Freud, believed that dreams reflect the individual's lifelong drive for power and success. Carl Gustav Jung (1875-1961) was convinced that the symbolism contained in dreams reflected a wider collective unconsciousness and was common to all, regardless of race or culture.

There can be little doubt that dreams do have symbolic significance, and certain archetypal symbols are now quite generally accepted in the field of psychoanalysis. Applying knowledge of these archetypal symbols should do much to enlighten the individual as to the meaning of his or her dreams. Nevertheless, it is important to remember that dreams are very personal, and it is only in the knowledge of the dreamer's own mood and feelings, and also his or her own circumstances, past and present, that dreams become truly meaningful. The A-Z that follows will help you in the process of interpretation if you bear this in mind.

A

abandonment someone who dreams of being abandoned by close family may be experiencing greater personal and sexual freedom than he or she has had before. Dreams of being abandoned may also reflect feelings of emotional isolation.

abduction if the dreamer is the abductor, the dream indicates a desire for power. Individuals who dream of being abducted are probably going through troublesome times.

abortion a dream of abortion dreamt by a man reflects feelings of guilt, not necessarily in connection with parenthood or actual abortion. When dreamt by a woman, abortion dreams can indicate anxiety about starting out on something new.

abroad a dream of foreign travel may represent the dreamer's desire to be free of the constraints of his or her present environment, whether by making new friends or significantly altering his or her lifestyle.

abyss if the dream involves feelings of fear, then it probably represents some loss of control, death or failure, or it may symbolize the dreamer's failure to face up to certain situations. If no fear is present, then a dream of falling into an abyss can represent the potential of going beyond preconceptions and experience. *See also* PRECIPICE

accident obviously, such a dream could have a link with a real accident experienced by the dreamer, but if no such experience has taken place, then the dream is probably due to anxiety. A dream of an accident at sea, for example, can signify the end of a long-term relationship and the accompanying feelings of insecurity. If someone dreams of coming to grief in an accident it may be that he or she is in fact punishing him or herself for something. Dreaming of an accident befalling somebody else may be indicative of negative feelings towards that person.

acid dreaming of acid may indicate that something is weighing heavily on the dreamer's conscience, i.e. 'burning into' his or her mind.

acorns the saying about great oak trees growing from little acorns has some validity in the world of dreams, where the acorn is a symbol of potential for great growth, whether it be mental, physical or spiritual.

acting dreams of acting and giving a poor performance suggest a lack of self-confidence. Dreams of performing may also point to the part that a person plays in life, the act he or she puts on in front of other people.

actions what one is doing with one's body in a dream may be significant.

dancing may represent the rhythmical movements of sex.

kneeling may denote a feeling of humility or even worthlessness on the part of the dreamer.

lying down may suggest relaxation, passivity, or a denial of responsibilities.

running may suggest a strong sensation of the life force within, and exuberance. Running away suggests avoidance, either of emotions, fears or responsibilities, depending on the context of the dream.

turning turning round and round in circles suggests

indecision and lack of direction. Turning to face in another direction suggests a decision to make changes.

admiration/adoration to admire others in a dream will not necessarily represent admiration of any one person in real life; it is more likely to represent finding and submitting to some sort of guiding spirit or influence.

adultery/affairs a dream of adultery may relate to a similar situation in real life, or may merely be a sign of unresolved guilt about something completely unrelated. Occasionally, dreams of committing adultery may be indicative of a simple yearning to do just that, but they may also indicate anxiety. A dream of adultery committed by one's spouse may reflect fears of just such a thing, or may reflect the dreamer's fears of his or her sexual allure.

adventure the adventures that occur in dreams are often a simple release from the reality of our lives, which is usually rather more mundane. If the adventure is terrifying, this normally reflects a desire to escape from a restrictive situation, while being afraid to do so.

aeroplane journey *see* JOURNEY.

afternoon *see* TIME

aggression/hostility to dream of being an aggressor is quite often a simple expression of anger that the dreamer has been forced to suppress in waking life, and it is worth reflecting upon why the dream anger is directed towards a particular person or group of people. A woman who dreams of an aggressive man may have a deep-seated fear of sexual assault, while an aggressive woman in a man's dream may, in reality, be a symbol for the unresolved fear of his mother.

alcohol dreams of being drunk and incapable may point to excesses of some sort in the life of the dreamer, or may express a subconscious fear of losing control.

angel an angel appearing in a dream is possibly a symbol for the mother of the dreamer, or at least those aspects of the dreamer's mother that exercised a benevolent or benign influence over his or her life.

animals dreams of animals may often be a reflection of 'the animal within' the dreamer, i.e. those motivations and impulses that are of an instinctive rather than an intellectual nature.

baby animals all of us still have certain needs for nurturing that we never grow out of. We all need to be cared for, to a certain extent. These needs are often represented by baby animals in dreams. Alternatively, baby animals could represent immaturity.

bear a bear may be a symbol of motherhood, or perhaps possessiveness.

bull the bull represents urges of a sexual nature, i.e. animal lust and aggressive impulsiveness.

cat cats symbolize the elegant and mysterious aspects of some people. Cats also represent intuitiveness.

dog dogs appear quite frequently in people's dreams. Friendly dogs can represent faithfulness and friendship, either of the dreamer or another person, whilst vicious dogs can represent aggression and betrayal.

donkey/ass the most basic life-force within the dreamer, i.e. the reflexes that are necessary for life, may be represented by an ass or a donkey.

horse the appearance of a horse in a dream is generally thought to represent human dynamic energy, whether mental or physical, sexual or creative. A wounded or a dying horse will therefore represent the weakening or fading of power in some way. Dreaming of running away from a horse or horses can mean a fear of the dreamer's own potential in some way, whether this be his or her sexuality or intellectual, spiritual or physical potential.

lion lions mean power, particularly the power and strength brought on by anger and aggression.

snake could reflect fears of plots against the dreamer or sexual anxiety.

anniversary dreams these usually indicate a happy time within the family, a get-together or a reunion.

anus *see* BODY.

appetite generally sexually orientated; dreams of loss of appetite can mean loss of libido, while hunger or thirst represent great sexual desire.

applause/accolades this is generally a wish-fulfilment dream. The dreamer seeks recognition for something which he or she has achieved. Some would believe that such a dream can foretell good fortune of some kind.

arms *see* BODY.

B

baby babies appear quite frequently in dreams. A crying baby is generally thought to represent illness of some kind. Babies also represent one's responsibilities.

Dreaming of looking after a baby and something dreadful happening to it can mean that you are frightened of making a mess of things. Dreaming of giving a baby to someone else to look after will mean shedding one's responsibilities, delegating, or perhaps even letting someone else take the blame.

baby animals *see* ANIMALS.

bag *see* SACK.

bath baths generally represent a kind of moral cleansing, a 'washing away of guilt'. The dreamer may desire to alter his or her habits and adopt a healthier lifestyle.

battle battle, or taking part in battles, usually signifies struggles that the dreamer faces in his or her life.

bear *see* ANIMALS.

bed *see* FURNITURE.

bedroom *see* HOUSE.

behind *see* POSITION.

bells bells are usually alarm bells, warning the dreamer of something he or she should be paying heed to, or something that he or she is in danger of overlooking.

bicycle journey *see* JOURNEY.

birds birds can signify many things in dreams. Birds in general are thought to represent some aspects of the human being, particularly intellect and spirituality. Some would say that a bird in flight represents sexuality, particularly sexual freedom.

birds in cages represent frustration and confinement.

crow represents death.

dove the symbol of peace in dreams, just as in life.

eagle power, freedom, perception and domination.

birth dreams of birth taking place can mean some sort of fresh start or major change in the life of the dreamer. For a woman, dreams of giving birth may be simply wish-fulfilment.

birthday dreams of birthdays represent happiness or good fortune.

black, blue *see* COLOURS.

blood *see* BODY

boat journey *see* JOURNEY

body the body is generally considered to be representative of the individual. Parts of the body therefore represent aspects of that person.

anus represents the individual's ability to express himself and to give of himself.

arms represent the potential in the individual for caring and affection.

blood can represent menstruation and thus womanhood, or the individual's essential being, the spirit that flows through him.

eyes are the perceptive abilities of the dreamer.

hands signify creativity, perhaps sexual creativity.

head is the idea that the dreamer has of him or herself, his or her intentions, wishes and beliefs.

mouth is representative of the dreamer's needs and their fulfilment. It may represent the female genitalia.

nose represents the intuitive qualities of the dreamer.

penis is the essential being of the man, the driving force behind his existence.

teeth are the things with which we bite, and therefore the dreamer's ability to be aggressive. Dreams of teeth falling out indicate a fear of loss of power and of growing old and dying.

vagina represents womanhood, femininity and procreative abilities.

book books in dreams represent wisdom and learning. A book that cannot be opened will signify a secret that cannot be revealed. Open books mean opportunities for learning and changes for the better in one's life.

box a box can signify a coffin and death.

bride/bridegroom the appearance of a bride or bridegroom in a dream will tell the dreamer something about his or her thoughts in relation to finding a lifelong partner.

bridge bridges in dreams will often signify a change or transition of some sort. Thus, crossing a bridge can mean making a major change in one's life.

brown *see* COLOURS.

bull *see* ANIMALS.

burglary dreaming of being burgled often means a fear of losing something precious, either something material such as one's home, or something more metaphysical, such as one's independence or self-confidence.

C

cage cages, and things in cages, generally represent restrictions or frustrations to individuals, perhaps to their ambitions or their sexual desires. *See also* BIRDS; ENCLOSURE.

candle men who dream of flickering candles may have concerns about their sexual potency.

Brightly burning candles may mean a desire on the part of the dreamer to find fulfilment in a spiritual way.

cannon *see* WEAPONS.

car journey *see* JOURNEY

castle castles represent security. The more heavily fortified the castle, the greater the dreamer's desire is for security. It may mean the protection of things that are important to dreamers or the protection of the dreamers themselves.

castration a man who dreams of castration undoubtedly has fears of failure and losing his status as a man. Women who dream of castration are probably embroiled in bitter relationships with men and seeking to disempower them in some way.

cat *see* ANIMALS.

cave the cave is often seen as the door to the subconscious; the further you go in, the closer you get to your individual subconscious being.

cellar *see* HOUSE.

cemeteries cemeteries represent what has gone before; this may in fact be dead people or figures from the past, or it may be a period in the individual's life, or one small incident that is over and done with. Dreams of cemeteries are also prompting the dreamer to think of death and the afterlife and, therefore, spirituality and religious beliefs.

chair *see* FURNITURE.

chess *see* GAMES

climbing someone who dreams of climbing is striving hard towards something in life.

closeness *see* POSITION.

clothes clothes in dreams may represent the way in which the dreamer appears to the world and to his or herself, his or her self-image and attitudes and the way in which he or she is seen in relationship to other people. Someone who dreams of being wrapped up in a large overcoat, for example, might be protecting, or seeking to protect, him or herself from others, or hiding some aspect of him or herself. Alternatively, such clothing may be representative of the loving protection that the dreamer feels from another, for example, a mother or a lover.

The *colours* of clothing may also be symbolic in dreams, just as we often dress in different colours according to our mood; thus, dark dreary colours can be symbolic of unpleasant feelings or occurrences, and black may symbolize death.

Underwear can symbolize the dreamer's feelings about his or her sexuality.

colours it is possible to dream in vivid technicolour, muted colours or monochrome, or one may have a dream in which one colour predominates, most commonly white or black. The colours in a dream can have considerable significance, depending on the state of mind of the dreamer and the context of the dream. *See also* CLOTHES.

black is the colour of the dark, hidden, gloomy and secret; it may be symbolic of death or of a fear of death. The dreamer may be feeling sad or depressed.

blue is quite a spiritual colour, it may symbolize hope, faithfulness, or may represent reasoning and higher intellect. A predominance of dark and/or dull blues, however, can signify depression.

brown is associated with excrement, dreariness and depression, but also with money, or even gold.

green is associated with growth, both physical and spiritual, and also with things that grow.

red is associated with anger, danger and warning. It may also be a symbol of sexual arousal in certain contexts.

white is associated with purity, cleanliness and innocence. It also has connections with illumination of the mind. White liquid, in certain contexts, may symbolize semen.

conflict any sort of conflict that is dreamt about has to be considered in the light of what is going on in the life of the dreamer. Victory in conflict, while dreaming, may be wish-fulfilment and some sort of compensation for the individual's inability to overcome a struggle in daily life.

corridor dreams about buildings or parts of buildings, such as corridors, are often very symbolic. The corridor may be interpreted as the birth canal, a passage from one stage of life to another, or a means of escape from a particular situation.

crossroads dreaming of crossroads may have associations with taking major decisions in life and of making a selection between two or more options as to which course of action to take.

crow *see* BIRDS.

cupboards *see* FURNITURE; HOUSE.

D

dancing a dream involving dancing is generally taken to be symbolic of the interaction of people on an emotional or sexual level, even as the precursor to sexual intercourse. It can also reflect feelings of elation, joy or victory that the dreamer experiences in life.

danger dreaming of being in some sort of danger or of having a strong sense of danger is one of the ways in which particular anxieties may be manifested in dreams. This may be a fear of letting oneself go emotionally or sexually and therefore risking betrayal or loss, or it may be fear of coping with some hurdle that is being, or is about to be, encountered in life. Such dreams need to be considered closely in the light of what is going on in the dreamer's life and his or her own personal fears, whether acknowledged or hitherto subconscious.

darkness the darkness represents the unknown and also what is depressing, even feared. However, where darkness is dreamt of in association with feelings of warmth and comfort, it may be symbolic of the time before birth and the safety of the womb.

daylight, **daytime** *see* TIME

dead people when one dreams of a person who is already dead, one is likely to be trying to resolve feelings about that person that are as yet unresolved.

death dreaming of the death of someone may indicate feelings of anger towards that person, even a desire to sever relations with him or her and thus be free of them. It is not likely to mean, however, that the dreamer wishes the person dead.

Dreaming of one's own death may be an attempt to deal with one's own uncertainties and fears about death or it may signify a wish to free oneself of certain current responsibilities or problems.

déjà vu this means literally 'seen before', and is a phenomenon whereby the individual will recognize something that they encounter in life as having been seen in a dream before. In many cases the person or place will have been seen before but has simply not been remembered. Nevertheless, there are cases in which people will, for example, know what is about to happen or recognize where they are going on a journey because they remember similar events or places from their dream life. There is no simple explanation as to why this happens, but it is believed by some that feelings of déjà vu are connected with reincarnation and are not so much rooted in dreams as in a previous life of the individual concerned.

departure dreaming of leaving somewhere or somebody has significance in relation to changes in the life of the individual, a 'leaving behind' of old attitudes perhaps, or a major change in lifestyle.

descent dreams of going down from a high place towards the ground may be symbolic of a descent 'back down to earth' in terms of one's approach to life or some particular problem. Dreaming of descending into the depths of a tunnel or cave can either mean an attempt by the individual to reach deeper within the mind and increase self-awareness, or it may represent a returning to the experience of life within the womb.

distance *see* POSITION.

dog *see* ANIMALS.

donkey *see* ANIMALS.

doors doors in dreams can represent opportunities or paths available to the dreamer in life. Thus, a closed door may represent an option that is no longer available to the dreamer, while an open door beckons the dreamer to take a chance or to move forward into a new 'room' in life.

dove *see* BIRDS.

dreaming of a dream it may happen, particularly in unpleasant dreams, that dreamers 'interrupt themselves' to give themselves reassurance—'it's only a dream'—or to tell themselves, 'this has happened in a dream before'. It may be that what is being dreamt about is particularly hard for the dreamer to cope with, and therefore the unconscious mind is helping the dreamer to keep the dream safely within the confines of the dream world so that it does not have to be faced up to in 'real life'.

drowning *see* WATER.

E

eagle *see* BIRDS.

earth as the earth is the source for growth, so earth in dreams signifies where we are coming from, our family roots, and social background.

eating eating is seen as the satisfying of a hunger, of a sexual or emotional nature. The sharing of food in dreams may be symbolic of the giving and receiving of love, the sharing of affection and/or bodies.

eggs eggs are symbolic of the potential of the individual, which has yet been untapped.

eight *see* NUMBERS.

ejaculation ejaculation is the ultimate end of the sexual act, the final release. Dreams of ejaculation are undeniably sexual and probably represent wish-fulfilment. Ejaculation or, for the female, orgasm while asleep will indicate that the individual has been having a dream that is tied to his or her sexuality, though this may not be immediately apparent through the remembered content of the dream.

emotion remembering the emotions that were felt while dreaming is essential in unravelling the meaning behind the content of any dream.

enclosure dreams of being enclosed may have connections with the barriers that the individual puts up against the world, the protective 'shell' that is used as a barricade against fears or hurt.

If unpleasant feelings are felt, the dreamer could be facing restrictions to his or her actions and feelings in life and feeling frustrated because of this.

escape dreams of escape may represent a desire to find release from particular circumstances in one's life, or may mean a recovery from depression or even illness.

Dreaming of something escaping from you could be a reminder of something that has been overlooked, or a missed opportunity.

execution a person who dreams of his or her own

execution may be depressed and suffering from severely diminished self-esteem. This could be a way of seeking self-punishment.

evening dreams of evening may be symbolic of the 'setting of the sun' in one's life, i.e. approaching old age. Alternatively, they can represent times of peace and rest, the calm after the storm and the final relaxation after a period of struggle. *See also* TIME.

exams while exam dreams commonly start in adolescence (a period marked by real anxiety about school exams for most people) they can be repeated over and over again throughout the rest of the dreamer's life, almost always occurring at times of particular stress. The dreams have similar scenarios for most people_ turning up at an exam to find that it is not the exam that you have prepared for, looking at the exam paper and finding that it is written in some incomprehensible script or foreign language, discovering that you have to sit an exam for which you have attended no classes, etc. Such dreams are always a pointer to real-life stress and an indication to the dreamer that this stress is a problem that needs to be dealt with.

excrement excrement is thought by some to be symbolic of wealth. The link between excrement and wealth has its origins in the belief of early alchemists that all the necessary ingredients for making gold were to be found in faecal matter.

Dreaming of incontinence may indicate a fear of letting oneself go in some way, perhaps a fear of one's emotions.

Excrement in dreams can also signify feelings of

disgust towards the self or another, depending upon the context of the dream in which it appears.

explosion dreams of explosion can represent outbursts of anger from which the dreamer feels prevented or inhibited in real life. Such dreams may be symbolic of orgasm, ejaculation and the culmination of sexual desire.

eyes *see* BODY.

F

failure like exam dreams, dreams of failure are generally linked to fears and problems in the dreamer's life. The dreamer may be coming to realize that what he or she is striving for in real life is, in fact, impossible. However, the dream may simply be an expression of fears that the dreamer feels unable to admit to.

falling dreams of falling are quite common. Often the dreamer dreams of falling and then wakes up before hitting the ground. Falling can represent any one of several things. Where the dreamer falls and lands, the dream may be sexually related, the fall representing the act of intercourse. Alternatively, a fall in a dream may represent a 'fall from grace' in the dreamer's life; the dreamer has let him or herself down in some way. Approaching some sort of edge and falling over may indicate that the dreamer is heading for problems in life, whilst dreaming of being in danger from falling can mean that the dreamer has real fears of potential disaster.

falling leaves *see* TREE.

family for most people the attitudes and values that they grow up with are related to and even dependent on their family. Whether an individual grows up to accept or to reject the values and attitudes of his or her family, it is generally true to say that they have built up their own set of values based on what they have seen and learnt within the context of family life. Equally, the way in which an individual behaves in relation to other people will, in all probability, be rooted in the patterns of behaviour of his or her parents and siblings.

Family figures in dreams may well represent themselves, but they can also represent that part of the dreamer that has its foundations in that particular family member. Thus, a man may have a dream about his mother in which he is perhaps resolving some of his feelings towards her; this dream involves a straight representation of his mother. Or he may have a dream in which his mother represents, perhaps, the caring and nurturing aspect of himself.

Generalizations as to what the appearance of a family member in a dream might mean can have little meaning without first some knowledge of the context of the dream, the dreamer's background, and the influences that have come to bear on his or her life through the family.

Even the fact that an individual may lack a family background (in the traditional sense) is of relevance.

fear fear is like all the other emotions that we experience while dreaming in that it can give a real clue as to the dreamer's state of mind, or the dreamer's true response to a situation, or an occurrence in his or her life. Dreaming gives people an opportunity to express feelings that they might otherwise be unable to express properly. Thus, while a person may present a brave, cheerful or perhaps angry face to the world, in dreams he or she can express the fear that lies behind the outward persona. The content of a nightmare, therefore, is not necessarily as enlightening as the fear that has been felt by the person who has had the nightmare. *See also* MONSTER.

fighting dreams of fighting are indicative of internal emotional, sexual or moral conflict on the part of the dreamer. It may reflect the dreamer's struggle for independence or freedom from a particular situation.

fire fire can symbolize great passions; anger, a consuming desire for something, or, quite simply, lust. In certain contexts, fire can symbolize enlightenment.

fish fish in dreams represent the unconscious motivations or impulses of human beings, either individual or collective, and are often closely connected with the unconscious drive to procreate. Fish may represent unknown aspects of the self that are as yet undiscovered or not yet understood, or may symbolize a supreme being, such as the Christ figure. Dreaming of eating fish can be symbolic of an attempt to find the hidden self by delving deep into the unconscious.

five *see* NUMBERS.

flies *see* INSECTS.

floating dreaming of floating suggests a certain loss of control, involuntary or otherwise, and the idea of letting oneself be carried along by life rather than living it in a more active fashion.

flowers flowers in dreams will often have strong sexual meanings. In general, they are symbolic of life and growth; also of beauty, love and tenderness. More specifically, a blossoming flower may represent the female genitalia, a bud the penis or vagina. Damaged flowers may symbolize damaged innocence, loss of purity/virginity, while wilting flowers may indicate the decline of sexual/reproductive powers. *See also* TREE.

flying to dream of flying is to dream of release from the influences that are holding one back; these may be practical difficulties, such as lack of money, stifling of creativity in one's job, or family commitments. It could also indicate repressive emotions or a lack of belief in oneself. For some, dreaming of flying may indicate a desire for sexual release.

Flying signifies freedom and independence and also the ability to take a different view of the world and of other people.

fog dreaming of fog indicates a problem of perception for the dreamer and a need to look at something more closely in order to understand it fully.

food food represents nourishment, whether for the body, the mind or the spirit. Dreaming of eating food is symbolic, therefore, of satisfying some desire for nourishment of some sort. Thus, to dream of sharing a meal with someone may represent the sharing of mutual love and respect or it may represent the act of sexual nourishing, i.e. sexual intercourse.

foreign countries dreams of foreign lands may be indicative of new experiences in life.

four *see* NUMBERS.

fruit fruit, like flowers, are symbolically linked with life, growth and sex. Fruits, in particular, are associated with reproduction and coming to maturity or ripeness. Unripe fruit may represent sexual immaturity. *See also* TREE.

furniture/furnishings furniture in dreams may represent, in general, our emotional baggage, or the feelings and attitudes with which our lives have become furnished through our upbringing and our interaction with others.

More specifically, certain items of furniture are thought to be significant in their own way. A bed, for example, may represent one's life as one has made it and one's level of happiness within that life. It may symbolize relations with other people, sexual or otherwise according to the context, marriage, occupation, etc. In some cases, where the mood of the dream is depressing, a bed or lying in bed may signify illness or a need for peace and retreat from the pressures of the outside world. Dreaming of lying in bed and watching things going on all around can indicate a certain passivity in one's approach to life.

Cupboards or wardrobes often hold sexual significance; the cupboard can be the womb. Finding something in a cupboard may signify discovering some aspect of one's sexual self. Alternatively, the cupboard may simply represent the mind, the depths of the cupboard standing for the deepest recesses of the psyche. Locked cupboards indicate secrets, or hidden thoughts; an aspect of the self that is hidden from the world or that is unacknowledged by the individual.

Dreaming of sitting in a chair may reflect a rather passive role in life for the dreamer, or a relaxed attitude.

future dreaming of events that are about to happen is a phenomenon that is much written about but little understood. It is believed by some to be a manifestation of the subconscious link between human beings, whereby strong feelings towards a person may give us an insight into the direction his or her life is taking them. However, this does not fully explain such dreams, as some dreams like this are not about people who are linked to the dreamer in any obvious way. Cynics would explain the phenomenon as being no more than coincidence.

G

gambling *see* GAMES.

games games in dreams can reflect the individual's attitude to life and the strategies that he or she develops to cope with certain situations.

Competitive games can symbolize a sense of struggle within the dreamer, a feeling of having to overcome competition from others to achieve goals in life.

Games like chess are indicative of a more intellectual approach, a consideration of strategies to employ in working towards one's ends.

Dreaming of gambling may be indicative of a certain

recklessness in the general behaviour of the dreamer and can serve as a warning to change one's ways.

garden gardens in dreams represent the 'inner person', the feelings and ideas that 'grow' within the individual. Thus, an untidy garden can be seen as a mind that lacks order and perhaps suffers from indecision or lack of purpose; alternatively, it may represent a person who does not listen or pay attention to his or her inner self (i.e. a neglected garden equals a neglected self). A very tidy, symmetrically arranged garden might be seen as a sign of a highly ordered mind, very controlled, perhaps inhibited, while a beautiful garden can reflect a happy state of mind and contentment.

Some would say that a beautiful garden is a sign of great happiness to come in the future, while an overgrown or untidy garden points to aspects of the individual's life that need attention.

gate a gate, or gates, may be interpreted as the entrance to the dreamer's inner self, the way in to the unconscious motivations of the individual. To go through the gate is to take the opportunity to increase one's self-awareness.

A gate may also be seen as the way into the dreamer's conscious desires, the way to achieve his or her ultimate aims. The interpretation of the dream will very much, depend on whether the gate lies open or closed, what, if anything, is seen to lie beyond the gate, and how the dreamer feels about his or her life at the time of dreaming.

genitals genitals in dreams are often symbols of the

dreamer's sexual self; a woman, for example, may dream that she has a penis, and this could be interpreted as her experiencing the male part of herself.

ghosts ghosts in dreams may either represent the dreamer's individual self, memories of the past that may be tormenting the dreamer, or things that he or she may feel guilty about.

Dreaming of the ghost of a person who is well known to the dreamer may point to the fact that the dreamer is still influenced, whether consciously or subconsciously, by the attitudes and opinions which the dead person had.

giants giants frequently appear in the dreams of children; they most likely represent grown-ups (who *do* seem huge to young children). Adults who dream of giants are possibly harking back to their childhood; alternatively, and particularly if the dream is frightening, the giant may be like a monster and represent something of which the dreamer has a deep-seated fear and which looms large in his or her thoughts.

gifts the giving and receiving of gifts in dreams should not be seen in a material sense but as the giving and receiving of love or the sharing of thoughts and ideas, or even actions that have certain effects on people. What is given, of course, need not always be pleasant; a nasty gift could be interpreted as something hurtful that is done by the 'giver' in the dream to the 'receiver'.

God one need not be a religious person to dream of God, or even of meeting God in some shape or form. Someone who dreams of God may indeed be in the process of analysing his or her own religious beliefs in life, particularly in relation to life and death; nevertheless, the God in the dream may simply be representative of some figure of authority in the dreamer's life. This may reassure the dreamer that responsibility does not lie with him or her alone, i.e. the buck does not stop with him or her. Alternatively, it may act as a reminder to the dreamer that the power to change things, or the ultimate control, does not lie in his or her hands.

Lastly, the appearance of God in a dream can take the place, to a certain extent, of the dreamer's conscience, bringing to the dreamer's attention the moral responsibility that he or she must bear for his or her actions.

gold gold in dreams rarely foretells untold wealth. It is more likely to represent things of a metaphysical nature that one values in life. Thus, false or tarnished gold will stand for values that are not worth having.

grave dreams of graves may be indicative of the dreamer's coming to terms with his or her own mortality, or the grave in the dream may represent some aspect of the dreamer's life, or character, that has changed or been overcome.

green *see* COLOURS.

guilt like many emotions experienced while dreaming, the guilt that a dreamer is feeling may well be guilt that is being repressed, or should be felt, for the dreamer's thoughts, words or deeds in real life.

gun *see* WEAPONS

gypsies dreaming of gypsies may indicate an unexpressed desire for more freedom in life; this may be physical freedom or freedom of the intellect or the spirit.

H

hair someone who dreams of having long, free-flowing locks may have a deep yearning for more freedom then he or she currently has in real life.

hands *see* BODY.

head *see* BODY.

heat heat is generally thought to symbolize the heat of strong feelings, either sexual arousal, romantic love or perhaps anger; it should be considered within the context of the dream.

height dreams of being at a great height, possibly on top of a mountain or a particularly high building, point to feelings of isolation on the part of the dreamer. It may indicate achievement or success, but this could be success that makes the dreamer stand out from his or her peers. *See also* MOUNTAIN; POSITION.

Dreaming of looking up at something that is very high above may well indicate a feeling of smallness in the general scheme of things.

hermaphrodite dreaming of having the physical characteristics of both sexes is likely to be either an indication of a need to explore one's own sexuality or an expression, within the safety and privacy of one's dreams, of aspects of one's sexuality that one may well be prohibited from expressing, or too inhibited to express, in real life.

hiding a dreamer who hides may indeed be a dreamer who has something to hide, or who thinks he or she has something to hide. The dreamer may wish to hide his or her true feelings from someone, or may possess a characteristic of which he or she is ashamed. If the predominant emotion felt while dreaming of hiding is fear, then this may indicate that the dreamer is frightened of letting his or her true emotions be felt or shown.

hills climbing a hill in a dream is indicative of a struggle of some sort in real life, either to achieve something or simply to maintain the status quo. Going downhill at speed in a dream suggests a certain loss of control, or at least a feeling that one is losing control in real life.

Gently rolling, fertile-looking, green hills may have a sexual meaning, being suggestive in particular of the female body, the breasts and belly of a woman of child-bearing years.

holes holes in dreams very possibly have sexual significance, symbolizing in all probability the vagina and womb. Emerging from a hole may therefore be indicative of the process of being born, while entering a hole may be either an expression of desire to return to the safety of the womb or a symbol for the act of penetration in sexual intercourse.

Other interpretations of holes in dreams include death, the unknown and the subconscious.

To determine the significance of a hole in a dream, it must be considered along with the other elements of the dream and the dreamer's current life and mood.

home dreams of home may indicate security and contentment, or may have a much more sinister meaning; it all depends on the experiences that the dreamer has had of home.

homosexuality one does not have to be homosexual in order to dream that one is homosexual or taking part in a homosexual act. Dreams give us the opportunity to explore aspects of our personalities and our sexuality that we feel, for one reason or another, prevented from exploring in real life. Dreams of homosexual love may be wish-fulfilment but are not necessarily so. We all need the love of people of both sexes, and yet we may feel inhibited from acknowledging that what we need from people of our own sex is love, even if this is not sexual love but the love of friendship, brotherhood, sisterhood or the love between parents and children.

horror feelings of horror are, like any emotion that can be felt in a dream, genuine feelings. They should be validated, not in relation to the content of the dream, but in relation to that aspect of, or occurrence in, the life of the dreamer to which the dream is alluding.

horse *see* ANIMALS.

house the house in a dream is thought to be symbolic of the self, its separate rooms all representing aspects of the self. Thus, the cellar and cupboards are the 'hidden self', the deeper recesses of the mind, or the aspects of oneself that one keeps hidden from others. The bedroom can either be the parts of one's mind to which one retreats when stressed, or it can be the aspects of the self that one shares with few others; the intimate, sexual self. The kitchen is the source of all nourishment, the way in which one seeks and finds fulfilment of all needs, physical and mental. The walls of the house are one's mental protection against life.

hunger dreams of feeling hungry may point to some unfulfilled need in the dreamer's life.

I

ice ice is symbolic of physical or emotional coldness. It may point to lack of love or loss of libido. The dreamer should consider his or her life to try to understand where this coldness originates.

illness dreams of illness may be the dreamer's first 'admission' that all is not well. The problem is not so frequently a physical one as one within the mind. It is possible that the illness represents unpleasant feelings of some sort (guilt, loneliness, etc) that may have been festering for some time, or even depression.

Alternatively, to dream of being ill (and hence of needing to be cared for) can denote a need for attention, affection or real caring in the dreamer.

A dream of someone else being ill is possibly an exploration of the dreamer's feelings towards that person; the outcome of the 'illness', the dreamer's emotions and the part that he or she plays in the scenario will all, therefore, be of significance.

imprisonment the person who dreams of being imprisoned is very possibly suffering from restrictions to his or her independence in real life; problems such as restrictive family relationships (particularly those between parents and children), claustrophobic love affairs, or guilty feelings may be holding the dreamer back from gaining freedom of action, movement or even thought.

infection as in the case of illness dreams, dreams of infections such as boils or festering wounds may reflect something within the mind of the dreamer that is bothering him or her, thus 'infecting' his or her thoughts. This may be no more than an irritation that has to be dealt with, but it can also be something of a more serious nature; for example, guilty feelings or negative feelings towards another person for one reason or another.

insects depending on how the insects are perceived in the dream, the interpretation of their appearance can differ. Buzzing flies may represent nothing more than a nagging problem within the dreamer's mind. The appearance of insects accompanied by feelings of displeasure or disgust will therefore reflect something about which the dreamer is more troubled. The problem may be a sexual one, in that the dreamer may associate both insects and sex with feelings of distaste.

In some dreams, insects or small creatures may be representative of one's children; thus, the mother who dreams of insects flying away from her may be dealing with her feelings about her children gaining independence and leaving home.

invisible an invisible presence, i.e. someone or something that cannot be seen but that is nevertheless active within the dream, is possibly symbolic of some influential authority figure.

island an island may be a symbol of loneliness or a feeling of isolation on the part of the dreamer, or it may be interpreted as a desire to cut oneself off from others.

A third possible interpretation of the appearance of an island in a dream is that the island represents the unborn child, and the water surrounding the island stands for the amniotic fluid in which the foetus floats.

J

jailer dreams of imprisonment are symbolic of restrictions to the freedom of the individual. Therefore, a person appearing in the role of a jailer in a dream will stand for the source of that restriction. This is by no means necessarily another person; it may be the attitudes or inhibitions of the dreamer himself or herself.

jewels jewels or treasure appearing in a dream are unlikely to represent material fortune of any kind. They are more likely to stand for that which the dreamer holds to be valuable in life in a non-material sense, for example, moral values, freedom of thought and creativity, family or romantic love.

journey most obviously, dream journeys can represent the 'journey of life', or a particular stage in life, such as childhood or marriage. Thus a journey that is particularly hard will reflect a difficult period in life. To dream of passing through difficult territory and emerging into easy terrain can reflect a change for the better in life and the overcoming of past obstacles. Those who dream of losing their way and feel frightened and bewildered on their journey are perhaps lacking direction in their lives, or may feel that events are taking such a turn as to leave them without control.

aeroplane journeys may stand for a swift transition between one part of the dreamer's life and another.

bicycle can refer to a difficult phase of life that has to be overcome.

boat the extent of difficulty experienced in a dream of travelling by water can reflect the extent to which boundaries have arisen in the dreamers life.

car can be a symbol of desire or sexuality. There should be particular importance placed on whether the dreamer is driving or being driven, since this is a reflection on the dreamer's sense of independence.

judge and jury these are often symbolic of the way in which we judge ourselves and our own actions; alternatively, they can represent the influences that have shaped our personal morality.

jump a jump from one place to another may be interpreted as a chance that has been taken or that would be worthwhile taking in life. A failed jump represents either a fear of not succeeding in something or the realization that one has made an error in life.

K

key a key can indicate the solution to a problem, that which opens up the door to success. Alternatively, it may be that which has been keeping repressed emotions locked up within the dreamer. A third possible meaning for a key in a dream is sexual, the key possibly standing for the penis, and the keyhole representing the vagina.

killing to dream of killing someone is unlikely to mean that you wish anybody any real harm. It is more likely that the person who is being killed in the dream is a symbol for some aspect of the dreamer's self that he wishes to repress, change or eradicate. Thus, dreams of killing may indicate a feeling of self-loathing.

Dreaming of being killed may point to some factor in the dreamer's waking life that is in some way stifling the dreamer or making him or her feel helpless.

kiss a kiss in a dream may be seen in general as an acknowledgement or acceptance of something. Thus, a dream of kissing somebody goodbye can be read as the acknowledgement of the need for some sort of transition in the waking life of the dreamer.

kitchen *see* HOUSE.

kneeling *see* ACTIONS.

knife a knife in a dream is very possibly a sign of aggression on the part of the dreamer, a desire to inflict pain, although not necessarily physical pain, on somebody. A knife that is used against someone but that has no effect may reflect feelings of powerlessness or inadequacy on the part of the dreamer.

In certain contexts, a knife may represent the male libido or aggressive sexual feelings.

knots knots can be read as problems with which the dreamer is struggling in waking life. There may be a confusion of emotions concerning some aspect of the dreamer's life.

L

ladder the ladder may represent a path in life that the dreamer is about to take. Climbing a ladder in a dream suggests that the dreamer is aware that there are hazards that have to be faced if goals in life are to be attained.

Occasionally, a ladder may have sexual significance as a metaphor for an erection.

letter letters may be symbols of intuitive feelings; an unopened letter would therefore represent intuition that is denied or the dreamer 'not listening to his heart'. Opening letters represents the realization of certain feelings or the achievement of greater self-awareness.

In certain contexts, an unopened letter may be interpreted as either virginity (protected) or sexual immaturity, or sexual awareness that has yet to be aroused.

lion *see* ANIMALS

losing dreams of losing things may reflect some sense of loss that the dreamer is feeling; for example, childhood may be now a thing of the past, or a love affair may be over.

In some cases the dream may indicate that a good opportunity may be, or already has been, missed.

lost dreaming of being lost indicates a certain sense of confusion in the dreamer's mind, a lack of direction in life, perhaps, or mixed feelings towards a particular person or situation.

love all emotions that are felt in dreams are genuine emotions; what has to be decided is whether the love that is felt in the dream is a compensation for that which is deficient in waking life, i.e. wish-fulfilment or a reflection of something that the dreamer feels in waking life yet has not acknowledged.

luggage luggage in dreams may be interpreted as 'emotional baggage', i.e. thoughts and feelings that the dreamer carries about and cannot, or will not, let go of.

lying down *see* ACTIONS.

lying in bed *see* BED.

M

machine machines can be interpreted as that which drives the individual, both in a physical sense (the heart, brain, hormones, etc) and also in a psychological sense (the wishes, desires and emotions which motivate the individual).

maggots as is the case with dreams of infections, illnesses, insects, etc, dreams of maggots point to some intuitive feeling that the dreamer has that something is not right; either something is causing mental disquiet, or some physical problem is requiring attention.

marriage in the case of a single person, a dream of marriage may be wish-fulfilment, but it can also be an exploration of one's feelings towards marriage, or a safe experiment with the concept.

Symbolically, marriage may represent the 'marriage' of two different, yet coexistent, parts of the self, such as the conscious and the unconscious, or the impulsive and the considerate. It could also mean the marriage between two personality attributes, such as gentleness and courage.

mask a mask is the face that the dreamer presents to the world; the secret or undiscovered aspects of his personality hide behind this.

A mask can also be a face that the individual adopts when coping with certain situations; thus, a soldier in battle will adopt the warrior mask. This is not his 'everyday' face, but, given the situation that is being faced, a genuine one nevertheless.

mattress a mattress may represent feelings of comfort and security or a relaxed approach, either to life in general or to a particular situation.

Mattresses can also function in dreams much as a bed, in that they may represent the dreamer's life as he or she has created it (the bed he has made to lie on). *See also* FURNITURE.

memory given that we spend so much time dreaming every night, it must be accepted that the great majority of our dreams are forgotten. This is not due to any failure on our part; a combination of circumstances conspires to erase most dreams from our minds. If time has passed between dreaming and waking, the mind may not be sufficiently focused to remember it. Some dreams are confusing and, therefore, difficult to recall with any degree of accuracy. Some dreams are simply too disturbing for the dreamer to confront in waking life and are consequently repressed by the subconscious.

menstruation a man who dreams of menstruation may be exploring his more creative, and productive aspects.

A woman who has ceased to menstruate but who dreams of menstruation may be having difficulties coming to terms with ageing and loss of fertility.

monster a monster almost always represents fear in a dream. This may be fear the dreamer has of something within him or herself, such as an obsession or an overriding passion, or it may be fear of something that one does not understand properly, such as love or death.

mountain mountains can be construed as obstacles in one's path, difficulties that loom large ahead.

mouth *see* BODY.

mud dreams of mud, accompanied by feelings of repulsion, suggest guilt feelings on the part of the dreamer, or a deep-seated belief that something is 'dirty' in sexual terms. Feeling 'soiled' by mud in a dream may suggest depression in the dreamer, while dreaming of sinking in mud or quicksand might suggest feelings of powerlessness or despair in the dreamer's waking life.

murder committing murder, or desiring to commit murder, in a dream points to the expression in dream life of strong feelings that are repressed in waking life. This is often sexual desire but may also be emotions that the dreamer is unable to express satisfactorily.

music the playing of music in a dream suggests self-expression. Thus, the person who dreams that he or she can suddenly play beautiful music on an instrument may be fulfilling a waking desire to be able to give vent to certain feelings or to use his or her creative talents.

N

night *see* TIME.

nightmares the content of a nightmare comes second in importance to the fear that the dreamer necessarily feels while having the nightmare. That is to say that any interpretation of the nightmare has to acknowledge first that the fear is genuine and that it will be reflected in some way in the dreamer's waking thoughts. If the source of this fear in waking life can be pinpointed, (fear of death, fear of one's sexuality, etc) then the interpretation of the other elements of the nightmare will be more straightforward.

nine *see* NUMBERS.

nose *see* BODY.

numbers numbers in dreams can be meaningful in relation to the person who is dreaming; for example, two may be significant to a person who has two children. Numbers are also imbued with a more general symbolism.

one may mean unity, wholeness, or the self. In some cases it may be a symbol for the phallus, or represent the male.

two can mean balance between two things, a complementary relationship, two alternatives that are open, or two things that are in opposition.

three may symbolize the genitals of the male, the threesome of two parents and child, or the Trinity.

four may stand for stability and the status quo, the

four seasons and the four elements being an essential part of the world as we know it to be.

five represents the human body—five fingers, five toes, five senses, the combination of head, arms and legs.

six is associated with balance, and occasionally sex.

seven represents spirituality or something that is sacred.

eight is symbolic of death and rebirth or resurrection.

nine is a symbol of pregnancy.

ten is a symbol of male and female as one.

twelve is a symbol of time or the whole year.

twenty-four is a symbol of the cycle of night and day.

zero may be a symbol for the female.

nurse a nurse is a symbol of caring, a dream of being tended by a nurse may be compensation for love that is felt to be lacking in waking life. The caring or nurturing may occasionally have sexual significance.

O

oasis an oasis in a dream may symbolize something, particularly an emotion, that has been missing in the dreamer's life and without which he or she feels barren.

obstacles obstacles that the dreamer encounters in dream life will be reflected by inhibitions, uncertainties or restrictions in waking life.

Confronting an obstacle in a dream may point to a need for the dreamer to overcome a fear in waking life.

ocean *see* WATER.

ogre dreams of encounters with ogres will often be an expression of the dreamer's attitudes to authority, or perhaps a father figure.

oil dreaming of oil may indicate a need to 'lubricate' a relationship in order to keep it running along smoothly, whether by adopting peacekeeping tactics in a difference of opinion or by suppressing one's own feelings in order to keep things on an even keel.

one *see* NUMBERS.

orchestra an orchestra playing harmoniously is indicative of the elements in the waking life of the dreamer working together to create a satisfying and harmonious whole. More specifically, it can be a sign of a contented relationship with oneself.

oven an oven may represent pregnancy or the womb. It may also represent one's ability to change as one grows and develops.

P

packing packing in a dream indicates a desire that the dreamer has for a change of some sort, getting away from old circumstances and emotions, possibly fulfilling a need for freedom. Dreaming that one is having difficulty in making up one's mind what to pack, or finding it hard to close the suitcase, would therefore indicate that the dreamer is as yet mentally unprepared for the changes that lie in store.

panic panic felt by dreaming will have its origin in

something in the dreamer's life that is causing similar feelings that need to be dealt with.

paper writing paper that has not been written on may represent things that have gone unsaid or feelings that have not been expressed by the dreamer.

Wrapping paper can be construed, in certain contexts, as either the dreamer's protection against the world, or the persona he or she adopts to show to the world.

paralysis dreams of paralysis may be a reflection of the way in which the dreamer is feeling in waking life—unable to function properly, helpless, etc. They may, however, in a semi-wakened state, merely be a subconscious acknowledgement of the fact that while the individual is dreaming, the major muscle groups are rendered inactive.

parcel parcels can be interpreted in a similar fashion to letters. An unopened parcel or package is indicative of feelings yet to be explored or self-knowledge yet to be acquired.

parents parents in dreams rarely represent real parents, rather the male and female aspects of the dreamer's nature, i.e. the man and woman who are within everybody.

past we may dream of people and things from our past in order to try to recreate the way in which we felt at that time, or alternatively, in order to work out unresolved inner conflicts about those times and to express emotions that have been previously repressed.

path a difficult, narrow, treacherous or winding path will point to troubles in waking life. A smooth, well-trodden path will indicate that the dreamer is adopting a 'safe' approach to life, following in the footsteps of others perhaps.

pen, pencil pens and pencils are means of communication. Occasionally, a pen or a pencil may act as a dream metaphor for the male sexual organ.

penis *see* BODY.

performing *see* ACTING.

pets dreams of puppies or kittens may not so much reflect a woman's desire to own a cute baby animal as to have a child of her own. *See also* ANIMALS.

photographs photographs are images; a photograph of the past in a dream represents the dreamer's image of the past, while a photo of the dreamer him or herself will represent the dreamer's self-image.

pill we take medicine because we believe it is doing us good and not because we like the taste. Similarly, dreaming of swallowing pills would indicate that the dreamer is doing something in waking life not because he or she wishes to do it but because he or she feels it to be necessary, either good for the dreamer, or a good thing to do in a moral sense.

place the place in which the dream scenario plays out will do much to reflect the dreamer's state of mind or mood in waking life.

ploughing ploughing is generally seen as a symbol of sexual intercourse, the preparing of fertile ground, the sowing of the seed, etc.

pole the most obvious interpretation of a pole or anything similar in shape that appears in a dream is a sexual one, i.e. that the pole represents the male organ.

pool *see* WATER.

position one's position in a dream, in particular in relation to other people in the dream, will be significant in terms of one's position in life, i.e. how one sees oneself in relation to the world with respect not only to station, but also to time, morality and beliefs.

closeness either stands for intimacy, someone the dreamer feels close to, or an idea or value which he or she holds dear.

distance denotes something from which the dreamer feels remote. This may be an unachievable aim or a set of beliefs from which he or she feels detached.

height dreaming that one is above something or someone, looking down upon them, may indicate a feeling of moral or intellectual superiority that the dreamer has. It might also mean that the dreamer feels that he or she has 'risen above' certain difficulties in life.

Where the individual dreams of being at a lower level, looking up at things or people, these things or people may represent higher ideals to which the dreamer aspires, or, in some contexts, an authority, a superior being or a God.

in front/behind generally speaking, things that lie behind the dreamer may be interpreted as things or ideas of the past which have now been left behind. What lies in front of the dreamer is, therefore, the future.

precipice dreaming of standing at the top of a precipice suggests fear of 'taking the plunge', i.e. fear of failure.

Falling off the edge of a precipice may be either a feeling of loss of control in waking life, or a symbol of death or what is not understood. Being trapped at the bottom of a precipice in a dream would suggest that the dreamer feels helpless and trapped in his or her present situation.

presents presents in dreams may represent affection in real life. *See ALSO* GIFTS.

prison *see* IMPRISONMENT.

prize dreaming of receiving a prize may indicate a wish for recognition in the waking life of the dreamer.

prostitution dreams of prostitution are generally indicative of some sexual need. A man who dreams of being with a prostitute may be seeking pure sexual gratification, without the need for emotional attachment. If the feeling of the dream is one of disgust, the man may want to express some aspect of his sexuality about which he feels ashamed.

Women who dream of prostitution may feel guilty about sex, or may have sexual needs that are not being met because they are being repressed.

punishment the person who dreams of dire punishments and retribution may well suffer from attacks of conscience in waking life, especially if his or her way of life is at odds with the set of morals he or she was brought up with.

quarrel dreams about quarrelling or fighting generally indicate that the dreamer is going through an internal struggle of some kind.

quayside departures from a quayside are indicative of

change in the life of the dreamer. One who dreams of taking leave at a quayside will very possibly be embarking on a significantly different stage in life.

Farewells at the quayside are acknowledgements of old ways and of thoughts being left behind.

quicksand *see* MUD.

R

race dreaming of taking part in a race suggests a sense of competitiveness, an awareness of one's position in life and, depending on the dream, either acknowledgement that one might not succeed or a sense of achievement at this particular stage in life.

Sometimes a race might indicate a particular rivalry in the dreamer's life.

radio this is generally a symbol for communication or, in some cases, intuition, i.e. an ability to pick up feelings 'in the air'.

railway generally symbolic of one's journey through life. *See also* JOURNEY; PATH.

rain dreams of torrential rain may point to feelings of depression or may indicate a cleansing process of some sort, i.e. a 'washing away' of guilt feelings or sadness, or a flood of long-repressed emotion.

The rain may have a refreshing quality to it and therefore represent some much needed change in the dreamer's life or spiritual wellbeing.

rape dreams of rape do not necessarily point to a fear of being raped (or of raping), nor do they point to desires on the dreamer's part. Rape is essentially violence, intrusion and abuse of power; dreams of rape are more likely to be exploring the dreamer's feelings in relation to these concepts rather than in relation to the rape itself.

recurring dreams it is quite common for people to begin having a certain dream fairly early on in life and then to continue having dreams that, even if they are not the same, are very similar in many ways, several times over a period of many years. The recurrence of dreams points to the recurrence of certain sorts of situations or emotions in the dreamer's life. The dreamer's reaction to, or way of coping with, the situation or emotion has altered little over the years and so the dream relating to the situation or emotion has remained, in essence, the same. When the dreamer matures or changes and ceases to react in this way then the dream will no longer occur or will be so different as to be unrecognizable.

red *see* COLOURS.

reflection you see yourself in a reflection, and so a reflection in a dream is the view that the dreamer holds of him or herself, i.e. it is his or her own self-image.

religion any individual, whether religious or otherwise, may dream of religious figures or religious imagery. The appearance of a religious figure, of God even, need not be related to religion in any way. For example, God may represent a figure of authority whom the dreamer respects deeply. Religious imagery may merely indicate that the dreamer needs to turn inwards more and to get in touch with the spiritual side of him or herself. *See also* GOD.

rock a rock may represent stability, 'down-to-earthness', or simply what is real.

rope depending upon the context of the dream, a rope may represent the umbilical cord, one's attachment to someone close, e.g. one's mother, or it may represent a restriction to the dreamer or the dreamer's own inhibitions in waking life.

running *see* ACTIONS.

S

sack/bag a sack is most commonly a symbol for the womb in a dream.

salt salt is what gives the dreamer's life its flavour, the dreamer's attitudes to situations encountered, the feelings sparked off through interaction with others, the influence and moods of those who surround the dreamer in daily life.

sand dreams of walking on sand, particularly deep, soft sand or sand dunes, reflect feelings of insecurity on the part of the dreamer.

school in dreams, school represents those values and restrictions that we impose on our own lives as a result of early experience.

sea *see* WATER.

searching dreams of searching might indicate some

feeling of loss in waking life, a loved one, perhaps, or one's childhood. Alternatively, it can indicate a search for a new path in life, that is, a new start. To dream of searching, but not finding, may indicate either that what is lost is lost forever or that the dreamer has some apprehension about finding what he or she is looking for.

seed seeds may simply represent parts of the human reproductive process, the sperm, or the egg. Alternatively, much like acorns, seeds can symbolize potential, either in people or situations.

seeing seeing is the sense that all sighted people predominantly use in their dreams, although their eyes are not functioning as they do in waking life.

The imagery and impressions that a dream leaves us with are translated into their sensory equivalents, and sight is the most common of these. Thus, our dreams offer us a panorama through which we can gain greater insight into aspects of our lives and our inner selves. Seeing things in dreams will offer the chance for the dreamer to see him or herself in a clearer light in real life.

seven *see* NUMBERS.

sex sex is a basic force that drives all humans; the human race needs to procreate in order to survive. Being a basic, primitive urge, it has come, through time, to be seen as somehow 'at odds' with the rational side of human beings. Animals are primitive, human beings have reasoning. Consequently, humans have imposed upon themselves certain restraints concerning sexual behaviour. These restraints are not universally the same, and it is true to say that for many people, their conditioning concerning sexual behaviour through family, religious authority, etc, may be completely at odds with his or her desires. Thus, sexual desires have to be sublimated in waking life.

The dream world is a safe place for the dreamer to explore feelings that he or she may feel prevented from expressing in waking life. Thus it can act as a release for sexual tension. Dreams of sex, or dreams in which sexual symbols occur (and there are many), can, if interpreted properly, offer considerable insight to the dreamer.

It must be added, however, that overtly sexual dreams can disturb some people and fill them with such feelings of guilt and revulsion that they try to sublimate the dreams themselves, instead of using the dream as a simple release or tool for building greater self-awareness.

shooting a shooting in a dream may be a metaphor for sexual assault. *See also* KILLING.

shrinking dreaming of shrinking is perhaps an expression of feelings of insignificance or humility.

sinking *see* WATER.

six *see* NUMBERS.

snake *see* ANIMALS.

stiffness someone who dreams of feeling stiff or being unable to move with any flexibility may, in waking life, be taking an attitude of inflexibleness about some situation.

sun the sun can represent warm feelings about something or towards someone, or it may symbolize enlightenment.

surroundings the surroundings or setting in which a dream is seen to be played out are often reflections of the dreamer's feelings. Thus, a sombre and dreary setting is likely to indicate depressed feelings on the dreamer's part, while bright colours will reflect feelings of happiness and contentment. A dream of cold surroundings, with snow and ice perhaps, can reflect emotional coldness or coldness of attitude, and a dream of a warm, safe environment will indicate that the dreamer probably feels quite secure and content.

T

talking talking in a dream may represent a deeper form of communication than talking in daily life.

Sometimes people dream that they try to talk but cannot get the words out, or find that all they can do is babble meaninglessly. This indicates that the dreamer is unable to express some feeling in waking life, or that he or she feels emotionally cut off from other people, misunderstood and frustrated.

teeth *see* BODY.

telephones telephones, and what is done with them in a dream, will reflect the dreamer's feelings about how he or she is able or unable to communicate his or her emotions to other people in waking life.

ten *see* NUMBERS.

tests dreaming of tests may be a reflection of the dreamer's awareness of being judged by his or her actions in daily life. They may also be general stress-induced anxiety dreams. *See* EXAMS.

three *see* NUMBERS.

tide *see* WATER.

time time can do strange things in dreams; we can find ourselves as an adult among the people and places of our childhood, and we can leap from one apparent time zone to another without disturbing the continuity of the dream. Certain times of day, however, are thought to have certain meanings within the world of dreams.

afternoon/evening may represent the later years of life.

daylight/daytime may represent the conscious self.

morning may represent childhood.

night its blackness may represent that which is unknown, perhaps that which lies in the future. According to the mood of the dream, night may represent a time of fear, or a time of peace and rest.

tools tools can often be interpreted as representing the male sexual organ in dreams. In certain contexts, when a tool is being used as a weapon, this may indicate hidden feelings of aggression, perhaps of a sexual nature.

touching touching can indicate satisfactory communication with others. Feeling oneself being touched may represent conscious awareness. Trying not to touch or be touched by somebody may indicate anger and perhaps a desire to detach oneself from him or her.

tower most obviously, a tower in a dream may have a phallic meaning; alternatively, it can reflect feelings of aloofness or of isolation.

treasure *see* JEWELS.

tree the tree can be understood to represent all aspects of our life. It is a manifestation of our growth and of where we are coming from. The tree roots represent our roots, and the branches represent the different aspects of our personalities and our direction in life. Its buds and new leaves represent new life; both that of future generations, and new life in the sense of spiritual renewal. Falling leaves are symbolic of that which is cast off from us, the things that we leave behind as we progress through life. The fruit of the tree stands for what we have created in life; our achievements, our children and our own selves can all be seen as our 'fruit'. The flowers of the tree may be seen as the human ability to procreate, or more specifically, female fertility. The bark of the tree is our protectiveness towards ourselves. The growth of the tree is a mirror for the growth of our bodies and spirits, and for the energy or life force that is necessary for that growth.

A dead tree seen in a dream may represent the death of a person, or the passing of something in your life.

tunnel to dream of crawling through a tunnel may indicate a subconscious wish for 'rebirth' of some sort, i.e. a fresh start. This tunnel symbolizes the birth canal.

A tunnel may also, in certain contexts, be interpreted as a passageway or a positive route from one phase of life to another. The transition or journey may not always be easy, but there is a 'light at the end of the tunnel' to motivate the dreamer.

turning *see* ACTIONS.

twelve, **twenty-four**, **two** *see* NUMBERS.

U

underground dreams of being underground may indicate a deep exploration of ourselves, or may point to a need to look more closely at the inner self.

Something buried underground may represent a secret, or an aspect of the self that is either repressed or hidden from the rest of the world.

underwear *see* CLOTHES

undressing a dream of undressing suggests the revelation of something that has been kept hidden, or a 'baring of the soul'. Thus it may suggest the giving of oneself in a certain sense, either sexual or spiritual.

V

vagina *see* BODY.

vampire images of vampires appearing in dreams may be provoked by Hallowe'en or scary films but not necessarily so. Dreaming of being attacked by a vampire suggests a feeling of being drained by another's dependency, or being weakened by another person's stronger will.

vanishing something that vanishes in a dream may be something or someone that has gone out of the dreamer's life, or it may be a lost opportunity. Somebody who dreams that he or she vanishes may be exploring the idea of death, or may have a poor self-image.

voyage *see* JOURNEY.

W

wall just as walls are built in real life to offer protection from the elements or from other people, so the wall in a dream can be read as a defensive image; it stands for the attitudes and postures we may adopt to protect ourselves and our feelings and the face we present to the world when we are sceptical. A wall that surrounds the dreamer may represent a feeling of being 'well-defended', i.e. a feeling of security. *See also* HOUSE.

wardrobe *see* FURNITURE.

water water is essential to life and, therefore, inevitably has a certain importance in dreams.

Dreaming of the *sea* may indicate an awareness of the depth of our unconsciousness, the knowledge that our inner selves go much deeper than our immediate awareness.

The vastness of the sea or the ocean reflects the huge realm of the unconscious. To see surging *waves* in a dream may indicate a feeling in the dreamer of the life energies that flow within, the unknown forces between will and action, for example.

Waves, and the ebb and flow of the *tide*, may represent the ebb and flow of human emotions, from negative to positive and back again.

Images of swimming in a deep pool may represent a regressive wish on the part of the dreamer with the pool symbolizing the fluid within the womb. Consequently, to dream of coming out of a pool of water may be indicative of a new start in life, or a wish for such a thing.

To dream of drowning, if fear is present, may indicate a fear of death; to dream of simply sinking underwater, without any feelings of an unpleasant nature, may indicate either a wish to explore one's unconscious in more depth, or an exploration of the idea of death.

Images of washing in a dream may indicate a desire for moral or spiritual cleansing, or a feeling that one has been cleansed of a particular feeling or emotion.

waves *see* WATER.

weapons weapons are generally symbols of aggression, either sexual, emotional or physical. The situation and the type of weapon may give a clue as to the nature of the aggression (for example, a gun or a cannon may be symbols for the phallus; the discharge of these weapons representing ejaculation). *See also* KNIFE, AGGRESSION.

wedding dreams of a wedding in which the dreamer is the bride or the groom may be wish-fulfilment.

Alternatively, a wedding may indicate a close spiritual or emotional tie, in other words, 'a marriage of two minds'.

wheel the wheel may be an image of the life cycle, the continuum of birth, life and death. It may also represent one's fortune, like the spin of the roulette wheel.

white *see* COLOURS.

wind the wind is thought to represent the motivating forces and external influences that 'blow' us along in life, as distinct from conscious wishes and desires.

womb dreams of returning to the womb or dreams that contain symbols that may represent such a desire suggest either the dreamer's desire to be free of a sense of responsibility, to cease to be answerable for his or her actions, or the dreamer's desire for a sense of security that he or she feels is lacking in waking life.

wound a person who dreams of being wounded may have had some experience in the past from which he or she has not yet recovered mentally. A man who dreams of severe injury may have a fear of castration. Women may dream of menstruation as a wound, or the wound may represent loss of virginity (about which she possibly has negative feelings). Wounds may also represent emotional distress.

wrapping paper *see* PAPER.

writing paper *see* PAPER.

writing writing is generally a symbol for communication. *See also* TALKING.

Z

zero *see* NUMBERS.

zoo dreams of a zoo in which all the animals are contented and in which the mood is obviously optimistic, may indicate a desire, that the dreamer may not have expressed in waking life, to exist within the confines of a family unit or similar set-up.

Dreams of a more unpleasant nature, where the animals are distressed, would indicate unhappiness in the dreamer and a deep sense of frustration with his or her present situation in waking life.